TAMIL POETRY

for

DAILY LIFE

PRABINDH SUNDARESON

notionpress.com

INDIA · SINGAPORE · MALAYSIA

ISBN 979-8-89277-765-0

This book has been published with all efforts taken to make the material error-free after the consent of the author. However, the author and the publisher do not assume and hereby disclaim any liability to any party for any loss, damage, or disruption caused by errors or omissions, whether such errors or omissions result from negligence, accident, or any other cause.

While every effort has been made to avoid any mistake or omission, this publication is being sold on the condition and understanding that neither the author nor the publishers or printers would be liable in any manner to any person by reason of any mistake or omission in this publication or for any action taken or omitted to be taken or advice rendered or accepted on the basis of this work. For any defect in printing or binding the publishers will be liable only to replace the defective copy by another copy of this work then available.

Contents

Preface

Tamil language is blessed with a high pedestal to stand on, with tall contributions from poets, writers, and artists from time immemorial, showering us with powerful ideas that enrich life and make it interesting at the same time. The writings of Tamil poets particularly from the *Sangam* age have an inbuilt call for action and a goal of self-affirmation, rising above social and religious distinctions. This is much needed today where we live insulated lives, thinking only about the future.

It is the memory embedded in the language that accompanies us all through our lives, where we connect the past to the future, like a river flowing continuously from its source. Is it then not our duty to know and understand and embrace our collective memories, our history, that gives us our strength and identity, and apply in our lives?

Thus began the journey of this book, by undertaking a memory tour across several generations of word-of-mouth, rigorously documenting the colloquial sayings, verifying the words and updating mistakes that inadvertently creep in over several variations.

The narrative in the book is seen through the eyes of a wandering poet, growing up in a farm on the countryside, watching the joys and pains of life pass by, quoting appropriately from an infinite assortment of Tamil texts and poetry. Different perspectives are added by introducing a theatrical style of narration with interpretations. The interpreter's version in English is marked with (I) right after the original Tamil verse for each situation.

It is indeed challenging to find close English equivalents to some of the verses, and a translation can never match the joy of reading in one's native language, but I have pursued this dream with the hope that the next generation will be able to appreciate the beauty and breadth of Tamil literature through an unconventional narrative style.

முன்னுரை

தமிழ் புலவர்களின் படைப்புகள் தமிழ் மொழிக்கு ஒரு மேன்மையான இடத்தை கொடுத்தன என்று சொன்னால் அது மிகையாகாது. முக்கியமாக, சங்கப்புலவர்கள் எழுதிய நூல்களில், மனித எழுப்புதற்கான ஒரு அழைப்பை நாம் காண முடியும். எதிர்காலத்தைப்பற்றியே சிந்தித்து, ஒரு தனிமைப்படுத்தப்பட்ட வாழ்க்கை வாழும் இன்றைய சமுதாயத்தில், இந்த அழைப்பு மிக்க அவசியமானது. ஆனால் நமது கடந்த காலத்தைப் பற்றி ஏன் நாம் யோசிக்க வேண்டும் ?

முற்காலத்து தமிழ் காவியங்களை படிக்கும்பொழுதும், மூதாதையரின் வார்த்தைகளை நினைவு கூறும்பொழுதும், நம் உள்மனதில் நம்மை அறியாமலே ஓர் இன்ப காற்றின் ஸ்பரிசம் படருகின்றது. மறைந்து போன ஞாபகங்கள் ஒன்றொன்றாய் திரும்ப வருகின்றன. அப்படி தோன்றியவைகளை கோர்த்து வைத்து எழுதியதுதான் இந்த புத்தகம்.

நாம் இவற்றை ஆவணப்படுத்தவில்லை என்றால் காற்றில் எழுதிய வார்த்தைகள் போல அவை மறைந்து போய் விடும்.

பல உலகங்களுக்கு பயணம் சென்று வந்த ஒரு சிறந்த புலவரின் கண்ணோட்டத்தில் இந்த புத்தகம் எழுதப்பட்டுள்ளது. அவருடன் கூட செல்லும்

மொழிபெயர்ப்பாளர்கள் மற்றும் ஒரு மாற்று கண்ணோட்டத்தை கொடுக்கின்றனர். நம்முடனே கூட வந்து, நாம் பேசும் வார்த்தைகளை கூர்ந்து ஆராய்ந்து, மாற்று கருத்து சொல்லும் முறையில் ஒரு கவிதையை இப்படி வர்ணித்தால் எப்படி இருக்கும் என்றெண்ணினேன். அதன் பிறப்புதான் இந்த புத்தகம்.

சில தமிழ் வசனங்களுக்கு இணையான ஆங்கில வார்த்தைகளை கண்டுபிடிப்பது மிகவும் கடினமான காரியம். ஒருவரின் தாய்மொழியில் வாசிப்பதின் மகிழ்ச்சிக்கு ஒரு மொழிபெயர்ப்பு ஒருபோதும் ஈடு செய்யாது, ஆனாலும், நமக்கு அடுத்து வரும் தலைமுறையினர் தமிழ் மொழியின் அழகைப் பாராட்ட முடியும் என்ற நம்பிக்கையுடன் நான் இந்தக் கவிதைத் தொகுப்பை உருவாக்கியுள்ளேன்.

Dedication

This book would not have been possible without the support and inputs from my beautiful family. I dedicate this book to them, with a special mention to the elders in my family, particularly my mother Mrs Ruby Sundareson who continues to render yeoman service at the CSI Whitin Church Pasumalai, for remembering every detail of a past that tends to be forgotten easily. Thank you for opening my eyes to many worlds.

Any account of childhood memories will be incomplete without a reference to my alma mater, the esteemed *Madurai Nadar Uravinmurai Jayaraj Nadar Higher Secondary School, Madurai*. I dedicate this to the vision of the school founders, the then Headmaster of the school, Mr R Dhanasekaran, and the current Headmaster Mr D. Ramesh. Thank you for your leadership to inculcate discipline and purpose in a world filled with so many conflicts.

Like my previous books, proceeds from this book go into supporting the work done by exemplary institutions. The proceeds of this book help *"The Home of Hope"*, and *"Liza's Home"*, who work for marginalised women and children. Thank you Dr. Molly, Dr. SK Subramanian and Dr Deepa, Dr L Gunasekaran, for the exemplary work you do to bring brightness to this world.

Acknowledgements

This book would not have been possible without the inputs from open texts freely provided by Tamil scholars and enthusiasts. But even with all of the content, the verses and colloquial words would not have come alive without the collective memories from a number of people, including my parents and my beautiful family.

Tools including Google Translate have been extremely helpful in making Tamil input accessible. Highlighting a few books here, a translation of Tamil proverbs by *Rev. P. Percival*, available at *Project Madurai* website, *"Introduction to Tamil Poetry - A. Chidambaranatha Chettiar, 1958"* available online, and *"Thamizhaga Varalarum Panpaadum"* by Dr. A.K. Perumal, among others, gave precious insight on the contributions from various Tami poets and the timelines.

I sincerely hope the content in this book provides an alternative window into traditional Tamil texts and poetry, and has a tangible mapping to our daily life.

Any resemblance to real world situations, characters or personalities is entirely imaginary.

The Beginning

Like every new saga, a glorious new day dawns.

In the lush tree studded farm, as the chirping of the crickets fades away, a new sound fills the air as the morning call of the larks reaches a cacophony, as if every bird wants a photo-opportunity with the first rays of the sun.

Amid the din, a deep voice sings.

(Poet) காலமே நீ எழுந்து

கடவுளைத்துதி நன்று

கால தாமதம் நன்றன்று

என் மனமே

(I) Rise early my heart

Praise thy God

Do not be late

The melody of this timeless song stays in the air.

My eyes open and stare at the darkness of the ceiling, before realisation hits that I am still on the bed.

(I) Such a melody ! Who is singing ?

(I) It's coming from the radio *'da*. Wake up!

I run outside and stare at the commotion.

It is market day.

The soft footsteps of the busy workers gently remind me of the busy time ahead. The ripe mangoes are already packed and kept ready in large sturdy baskets (*Kadavam*) made of palm leaves, each holding a load of precious mangoes.

"Dey, come quick. If we are late, we have to stay longer to sell all of this..hurry up", a voice thunders.

Atleast, today I do not have to fill water from the well, pick up twigs, or dig up tapioca tubers.

Almost as an afterthought, the voice adds.

(I) *Finish the coffee before you start! It's the last tumbler on the table, for you!*

The hot coffee laced with milk and jaggery (*Karupatti*), strengthens my resolve, as I size up the one bag that I feel confident of carrying, pick it up and join the others trudging up the winding road toward the market (*Santhai*), breathing in the nippy early morning air already becoming warm, I walk up the long road until the raucous sound of the market reaches the ears.

Thus begins the day for the poet, at a farm in the remote corner of this universe.

Like the rays of the sun penetrating the darkness, with a keen eye for detail and a bag of Tamil texts, the poet soon joins the stream of life with a quick wit and a quicker pen.

His first stop, of course, is the place where everyone grows up.

Schooling

The poet crosses the wide tree studded ground of the school, and reaches the pillars of the main building, where he can hear the Headmaster thundering at a late-comer, and the office staff busy with their routine. The smell of diesel pervades the ground, as the old school bus affectionately called "dubby", puffs its way into the bay, and a never ending stream of children climb down and rush to their classes.

The emptiness of the large black board prominently stationed at the entrance seems to beckon a teacher. The poet watches as the teacher picks up the white chalk kept in a small ledge at the bottom, and begins to write. The letters begin to appear, as if by magic.

The poet reads.

(Poet) பள்ளியால் எனக்குப் பெருமை

என்னால் பள்ளிக்குப் பெருமை

(I) I am proud of my school

My school is proud of me

The beautiful verse illustrates how a child, as a student, is proud of studying in this school. Later, the alumni make the school proud. The poet adds.

(Poet) ஊருக்கு ராஜாவானாலும் அவன்

பள்ளிக்கு பிள்ளை தான்

This exemplifies the eternal superiority of the school we enter as a kid, and walk out as individuals, ready to take on the world.

(I) The king of the land

Is still a student in his school

Importance of Education

The poet sees a man fighting furiously with his father. The man argues that he was not brought up properly, that his father did not teach him the tools required for him to succeed as an adult, specifically, by not sending him to school.

The poet quotes this scenario from *Agathiyar* (*அகத்தியர்*).

(Poet) கொள்ளிக்கும், நீ பட்ட கடனுக்கும் எனை குறித்ததல்லால்

துள்ளித்திரிகின்ற பருவத்தில் என் துடுக்கடக்கி

பள்ளிக்கு வைத்திலையே தந்தையாகிய பாதகனே

(I) O spiteful man, my father,

You marked me for suffering,

For taking care of you,

And for clearing your debts,

But not to teach me obedience,

Or showing me the way to the school

The Way of the Stick

A group of children playing in an empty ground, surrounded by trees.

Someone shouts, "*It is already dark, time to go home*"

Everyone scatters.

The child tiptoes into the verandah of his house (*Mattupah*), hoping no one notices. The reasons are many. The long stick (பிரம்பு) in the corner of Grandpa's room stares at him, waiting for the magic word to be spoken, or else…

"*Shh…*" the boy whooshes, as he successfully navigates to his room without anyone noticing.

Not finishing the food on time, staying out after evening time, or missing out on homework, all invite the wrath of the elders. A rap with a long stick, usually in the back of the leg, sets a bitter flag in the mind of the child, never to repeat the mistake again.

After several hours, the parent or grandparent placates the sulking child, giving a candy or two and explaining why a punishment is necessary.

The poet sums up this situation.

(Poet) அடி செய்யும் உதவி

அண்ணன் தம்பி செய்ய மாட்டான்

(I) The good from a spanking

Not even brothers can match

Circle of Life

Though many things change in the world, the family is still the fundamental unit of life, an indivisible and invisible entity holding together multiple people, chugging together in spite of various challenges to togetherness, providing a space for everyone including the little ones and the elderly. Children have a great say in families due to their very nature, of not knowing rules or which rules to obey, until they become more obedient later on.

The poet sees lion cubs playing with the father, rolling, kicking and biting him. The big lion braves all of it. A lion cub is not afraid of his father, though the father is the ferocious lion and king of the forest.

(Poet) கொல்லும் சிங்கமானாலும் குட்டிகள் அஞ்சுமோ

(I) Though he may be the ferocious lion

Will his cubs fear him ?

Learning When Young

The poet observes that many of our personal traits do not change over a lifetime. Sometimes these are good habits, sometimes these are not worthy to be rigidly carried over. Hence we need to be aware of our own traits, and work towards adapting to new environments in a fast changing world. Some of them could be our strengths, and others might need to be discarded.

The poet says.

(*Poet*) ஐந்தில் வளையாதது

ஐம்பதில் வளையுமா

(I) *That which did not bend at five,*

Will it bend at fifty ?

Many qualities can be identified by children's behaviour when they are young. Some of them change over the course of time, but some do not.

(*Poet*) விளையும் பயிர் முளையில் தெரியும்

(I) *A plant is known*

When it emerges from its seed

(Poet) தொட்டில் பழக்கம் சுடுகாடு மட்டும்

(I) A trait stays

From the cradle to the grave

The best age for learning is when we are young. It is well proven that the development of a child's brain peaks around the age of ten. What we learn when young, gets cemented in our next phase of life. Hence it is important to teach children when they are young and when they are able to absorb good habits to their maximum potential.

(Poet) இளமையில் கல்வி

சிலையில் எழுத்து

(I) What is learnt when young

Is like a letter, sculpted on stone

The Taste of Mango

The taste of a mango expresses itself in various forms from pickles to raw mango to the ripe fruit itself, no wonder it is called the king of fruits. The poet observes that the taste of a mango can make a child eat any food that includes it, even if the child's mother is unable to make the child eat without the mango by singing lullabies, or showing them the moon, or other usual tricks.

Observing this ability of a mango, the poet says.

(Poet) மாதா ஊட்டாத சோற்றை

மாங்காய் ஊட்டும்

(I) A child that refuses food

Even if it be from motherly good

Will wait eagerly for more

If it can smell the mango in store

Bitter is my Word

Elders have experience that can relate to the situation at hand. It is important to listen, and apply this knowledge in the appropriate context. In the eagerness of youth, many times the poet sees children not using these pieces of advice, but when looking back, the advice always seems right.

The poet says.

(Poet) மூத்தோர் சொல்லும் முது நெல்லிக்கனியும்

முந்தி கசக்கும் பிந்தி இனிக்கும்

(I) Words of elders, like a berry

Are bitter first, and sweeter later

(I) It pays to listen to elders.

Enabling Children

For every parent, their own children are the best in the world and they praise them to no end. It also helps children to fulfil their need for belonging. But sometimes, parents miss noticing their children's shortcomings and glorify them all the time instead of guiding them properly.

Hence the parents need to maintain a balance between giving the children enough freedom for them to grow, and teaching them the right things.

The poet notes.

(*Poet*) காக்கைக்கு தன் குஞ்சு பொன் குஞ்சு

(*I*) *A chick is golden, for even the (black) crow*

The other way round, the poet extols the children to respect their parents. This verse exemplifies the virtues of a mother and father, and the importance of listening to them, almost treating them as God.

(*Poet*) தாயிற்சிறந்த கோயிலும் இல்லை

தந்தை சொல் மிக்க மந்திரமும் இல்லை

(*I*) *No temple better than a mother*

No magic more powerful than the words of a father

When a child achieves greatness in some field, the child is recognised and praised by society for their deeds, and their parents get praised, for it is the parents' sacrifices that enabled their children to be so accomplished. Such praise is the greatest help (gift) that a child can give to the parent.

The poet says, quoting from *Thirukural*.

(Poet) மகன் தந்தைக்காற்றும் உதவி, இவன்

தந்தை என்நோற்றான் கொல் எனும் சொல்

(I) When others wonder

What penance did his father do, they ponder

To beget this wonderful human

That then, is the greatest help to the father, from his son

Mother and Child

A mother thinks about her children all the time. Seeing her children grow up gives her immense joy. But, when she hears someone else praising her child, she feels more joy than what she might have felt when she gave birth to the child.

The poet says.

(*Poet*) ஈன்ற பொழுதிற் பெரிதுவக்கும்

தன் மகனை சான்றோன் என கேட்ட தாய்

(I) A mother's joy knows no bound

When her son's praise is found

Even more happier than when

She delivered him from the womb

A cloth has the characteristics of the thread it is made of. Similarly, a child takes after its mother in its natural abilities, and nurture takes care of the rest.

The poet says this.

(*Poet*) தாயைப்போல் பிள்ளை

நூலைப்போல் சேலை

(I) Child follows the mother

Just like the thread and the drape

The affection a mother has for her child is incomparable to anything else. Across the world there are stories that imbibe this, including the Hebrew story of King Solomon the Wise, who has to find the real mother, when two women claim rights to a baby.

The wise King thunders - "Let the child be cut into equal halves, and let one half be given to each woman". As soon as he utters this order, a loud wail is heard. One of the women breaks down and offers to give away the child instead.

The wise King who now knows the real mother, orders the baby to be given to her.

The poet reinforces this with a saying,

(Poet) தாய் தன் சேயின் கையை சில நாட்களே பிடித்திருந்தாலும்

தன் மனதில் வாழ்நாளெல்லாம் வைத்திருப்பாள்

(I) Mothers hold their children's hand for a short time

But hold them in their hearts forever

Obedience

The poet walks inside an apartment complex, where children gather for playing as soon as school is over and after having refreshed themselves. An empty place outside the home becomes a noisy playground. The especially naughty ones make neighbour's lives miserable, particularly for elders, or those trying to work or attend conference phone calls for work. When several bouts of shouting at the children do not help, the affected parties accept failure, sighing. That's the best they can do, when faced with insolent kids who have to be chased away, again and again!

The poet hears the aggrieved neighbours hinting at the bad behaviour of the children to their parents.

(*Poet*) நல்ல மாட்டுக்கு ஒரு சூடு

(*I*) *A good animal needs only one brand*

(*I*) *Just yesterday I chase them away, and they are back!*

(*I*) *A tough animal can withstand a hot brand!*

(*I*) *Are they tough, or are they disobedient, only time will tell!*

False Affection

33

The poet sees little children calling their parents to carry them, instead of walking along on the road on their own feet. Is it because they are tired, afraid of something on the street, want a dose of affection, or just out of laziness ? On closer look, the poet sees the children calling out only to those who will yield to their request.

Likewise, in many situations, people approach only those who they know will respond to their request in a positive manner.

The poet says.

(Poet) எடுப்பார கண்டால் குடம் கூத்தாடும்

(I) The pitcher dances in merry

Seeing the one who will carry

Exams and War

Powerful kings defend their forts with valour and might, and they never lack weapons. But when they leave for war, they also need an emotional reminder - from their elders, their loved ones, amplifying the importance of "holding the fort" during a war.

The below is a friendly reminder to children, before embarking on a critical competitive task.

The poet says this colloquially.

(Poet) கோட்டையை விட்டு விடாதே

(I) Don't leave/lose the fort to the enemy

Tug of War

This verse describes a tug of war between two children. Both of them want the same thing, but both do not give up their grip, and the tussle continues.

The poet has chosen interesting names for them.

(Poet) விடாக்கொண்டான் கொடாக்கொண்டான்

(I) Won't give and won't leave

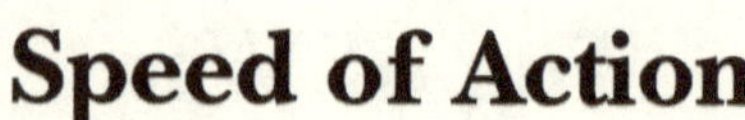

Speed of Action

The poet observes a man going speedily ahead. He hails him, and understands the reason for his pace, and smiles.

When going to a feast, be in the front of the queue. When going to a war, direct from the back.

The poet says.

(*Poet*) பந்திக்கு முந்து படைக்கு பிந்து

(*I*) *Lead the war from the back*

Lead the feast from the front

Avvaiyar'um Kambar'um

The poet happens to travel to the King's court along with the great poetess *Avvaiyar*, with the king known to patronise Tamil arts. *Kambar* is delighted at seeing his old friend, but he is more than delighted at seeing *Avvaiyar* with him, providing an opportunity for him to score points. Though *Kambar* is the royal poet, *Avvaiyar* bows to no one, including *Kambar*. Knowing *Avvaiyar's* character, *Kambar* decides to pose her a riddle that ridicules her at the same time.

Referring to *"Ara Keerai"* (*Amaranthus Dubius)* a very nutritious green that grows in South India, *Kambar* taunts the poetess with a short question that simultaneously tends to berate her, with an impolite address.

(Kambar)நாலிலை பந்தலடி, அது என்ன ?

(I) Four-leaf bloom, O'maiden, what may it be ?

The towering poetess *Avvaiyar* who is no stranger to *Kambar*, responds, nay, retorts with her own riposte, cloaking her anger and irritation with a mellifluous stream of words, equating *Kambar* to various low form of animals and figure(I) from a buffalo, to an unfinished house that has only walls, to monkeys, and ending with the expected answer. A befitting reply indeed!

*(Avvaiyar)*எட்டே கால் லட்சணமே

எமனேறும் பரியே

மட்டில் பெரியம்மை வாகனமே

கூரையில்லா வீடே

குலராமன் தூதுவனே

ஆரையடா சொன்னாய் நீ

(I) Oh you, ugliest of all

The beast of Yama,

Accompanying the cursed

Like a roofless house

Like a monkey, messenger of Rama

Aarai is your answer

The court applauds. The poet records this as one of his greatest moments, seeing the two poets taking Tamil poetry to great heights, individually, and collectively, even as they spar with each other verbally.

The poet praises the prodigy *Avvaiyar* and her contributions to Tamil poetry through this short verse.

(Poet) அவ்வை கிழவி நம் கிழவி

அமுதின் இனிய சொற்கிழவி

செவ்வை நெறிகள் பற்பலவும்

தெரியக்காட்டும் பழங்கிழவி

நெல்லிக்கனியை தின்றுலகில்

நீடு வாழும் தமிழ்க்கிழவி

வாழும் வாழ்வில் ஒரு நாளும்

மறவோம் மறவோம் மறவோமே

(I) Avvai, the grand old lady of ours

With words sweeter than Amirtham (an immortal treat)

So many great virtues

Pointed by her

With a worldly gooseberry

Living long, this grand old Lady

So long as we live

Let us not forget, not forget, not forget!

Reputation

Kambar is the court poet, and very accomplished in his art. His fame has spread far and wide. Legend goes that a poet from another part of India, wants to challenge him. The land is not well mapped, and the challenger lands in a nearby place, and asks for directions. As it happens, the poet is met by one of *Kambar's* staff, who offers to guide him to the famed poet's residence, if only he could answer his question. But the question is so cunningly worded, that the challenger is unable to answer.

He returns back, only with the knowledge that he could not even match wits with the great *Kambar's* servant.

When we work hard and achieve fame and strength, even our followers will be strong. The bar raises for the competition. Our reputation goes ahead of us.

The humbled poet now far away, having learnt his lesson, says this.

(*Poet*) கம்பர் வீட்டு கட்டுத்தறியும் கவி பாடும்

(*I*) *Even the pillars in the house of Kambar, will recite*

(*Poet*) கற்றது கைமண் அளவு

கல்லாதது உலகளவு

(I) What is learnt is but a handful,

What is yet to be learnt, is the world

Facing Obstacles

Wise people do not set themselves up for failure, do not keep thinking about failure, but look beyond, and fix the causes for failure. This paves the way for future success. Life can sometimes subject us to pushes and pulls from one, two, or many sides, but our focus should be on our goals.

The poet says, quoting from Tamil proverbs.

(*Poet*) பட்ட காலிலே படும்

கெட்ட குடியே கெடும்

(*I*) *The wounded leg will hurt again*

The fallen will fall again

The poet takes another example using the pestle (*Ural*) and Mathalam.

(*Poet*) உரலுக்கு ஒரு புறம் இடி

மத்தளத்துக்கு இரு புறமும் இடி

(*I*) *Ural gets hit at one end,*

The Mathalam gets hit at both ends

Focus

Even a rough edged hard stone gets smoothened by the continuous movement of a tiny weightless creature like an ant. The poet observes this, and says, irrespective of our size, we can make qualitative and quantitative changes by working continuously towards our goals.

(Poet) எறும்பு ஊர

கல்லும் தேயும்

(I) Even a stone may disappear

By the continuous crawling of ants

An Ammi (or ural, or a large thistle) is a very heavy stone used to powder rice, as it is built to handle the constant grinding operation. But if we keep pushing it, even this heavy stone is bound to move. This can be true for many things in life, and patience is key to achieving our objectives. The poet adds.

(Poet) அடி மேல் அடி வைத்தால்

அம்மியும் நகரும்

(I) Even a heavy stone will move, tap by tap

Unpredictable Life

The poet notes that nothing can be predicted in life. In the circle of life, anything is possible. So being prepared for the unknown is key!

Even if we slip and fall, we should be prepared to get up and walk again.

The poet says, quoting from Tamil proverbs.

(Poet) ஆனைக்கும் அடிசறுக்கும்

(I) Even an elephant may slip and fall

Inertia

While starting on a new task, particularly one not familiar to us, we plan ahead. But if we keep losing time while making a perfect plan, we cannot move forward at all. So we need to take a small risk, and take the leap of faith when we are reasonably confident. The poet says, there is no perfect plan, and there is no perfect time.

Inertia is to be overcome, and it can be overcome only if we have a strong motivation to get it done.

The poet says.

(Poet) திரை நீங்கி தீர்த்தம் ஆட முடியாது

(I) Do not wait long for the surf to clear, else we may never experience the water

(I) Waiting for the surf to cease and the wall of white to clear from the water, before taking a dip in the ocean, is meaningless.

Winning Ways

When life itself depends on the result of an action, the poet says, we should make sure that the action is successful. He illustrates this from the perspective of a milkman, who depends on the cow to provide him with milk that he can sell to earn his living. The milkman does everything he can, to do whatever it takes, to milk the cow.

The poet says,

(*Poet*) ஆடுற மாட்ட ஆடி கறக்கணும்

பாடுற மாட்ட பாடி கறக்கணும்

(I) Dance to the cow that dances

Sing to the cow that sings

Breaking Boundaries

In this verse, the poet compares the standard of a person not erudite in the ways of the world and not well educated, to a bird that spreads its wings claiming itself to be a peacock.

Quoting from Moothurai (மூதுரை) of Avvaiyar (ஒளவையார்), the poet says.

(*Poet*) கான மயிலாட கண்டிருந்த வான்கோழி

தானும் அது போல் பாவித்து

தன் பொல்லாச் சிறகை விரித்தாடினாற்போல்

கல்லாதான் கற்ற கவி

(I) Like the turkey that imitates a wild peacock's dance

And spreads its wings with an unpractised prance

So are the words of an uneducated person

They remain false, and stubborn

(I) But is this the fault of a Turkey ? It is also unwise, to compare a Turkey to a Peacock

(Poet) Many a time, we are conditioned to see beauty only in a peacock. But beauty and life exist in many forms, and we should break out of our preconceived boundaries, to be able to see the truth in its entirety.

Strategy

The poet notes that important things necessary for survival should be accessible quickly, in the event of emergencies.

Colloquially, the poet frames this by saying.

(Poet) தனக்கிருந்தா போதாது

அதுவும் தலைமாட்டில் இருக்கணும்

(I) Not enough if it is yours to heed

Things important should be close to your head in need

Hard Work

What are the qualities of hardworking people ?

The poet answers this, quoting from *Kumara Kurubarar,*

(*Poet*) மெய் வருத்தம் பாரார் பசி நோக்கார்

கண் துஞ்சார்

எவ்வவர் தீமையும் மேற்கொள்ளார்

செவ்வி அருமையும் பாரார், அவமதிப்பும் கொள்

கருமமே கண்ணா யினார்

(I) *They, who are focused on their work*

Do not feel hunger

Nor do they sleep whenever

Nor watch their enemies

Nor the time

Nor their sufferings, nor others mudslinging

Until the finishing line is seen

The poet notes, those who work hard, will always get their due, and will be praised for their diligence. Like the humble and hard working ant, a hard working person will be well regarded in society.

(Poet) முயற்சியுடையார் இகழ்ச்சியடையார்

(I) The one who put in hard work

Will never be disgraced

Perseverance

51

The poet has seen many, who have great belief in God. They believe that their wishes and prayers will be granted. But sometimes, even if God appears to disregard our direct prayers, working toward our goals diligently will yield results in the end.

The poet says, quoting from *Thirukural.*

(*Poet*) தெய்வம் தான் ஆகாதெனினும், முயற்சி

தன் மெய் வருந்த கூலி தரும்

(*I*) *Even if God has turned*

True hard work will succeed

Standing Out in a Crowd

When we attend a gathering, we should be introduced as a reputed person. Our reputation should precede us. If we are not well regarded in that community, it is better not to be present in that gathering at all.

The poet quotes from *Thirukural.*

(*Poet*) தோன்றிற் புகழோடு தோன்றுக அஃதிலார்

தோன்றலின் தோன்றாமை நன்று

(I) Be known and be announced

By those around

Else, better not be on that ground

Preparation is Key

53

While the poet has seen several bloody wars in his lifetime, he realises our generation has no chance to see wars on a large scale. But the leaders need to ensure that the troops and war machinery is always prepared, in the event of major changes in the world order, and to tackle perceived threats. Just the amount of preparation and the perceived strength of the troops is sometimes sufficient to avoid wars and direct combat.

In a similar manner, the poet advises children to always be prepared even if there is no upcoming exam. The exam is a war, and continuous preparation is key!

The poet says,

(Poet) The more you sweat in peace

The less you bleed in war

(I) அமைதியான காலத்தில் கடிந்து உழைத்தால்

போர்க்காலத்தில் இரத்தம் சிந்த தேவையில்லை

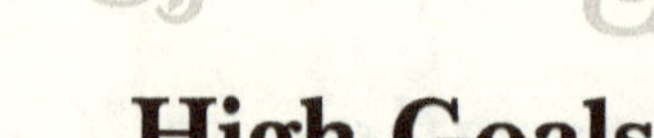

High Goals

The poet is now enamoured with reaching stars far beyond the solar system. He calculates the distance from the earth to the sun to be more than 100 million kilometres, while the stars in "Alpha Centauri" are more than 10 trillion kilometres away. The farther the celestial body, he notes it will take longer and involve more effort to reach.

What should be his target ? He thinks a while, and realises, dreams need to be big, and the results will follow.

Calling upon us for putting higher efforts and to aim high, the poet remembers this quote from *Norman Vincent Peale*.

(Poet) Aim for the stars. You will reach the sun.

(I) நட்சத்திரங்களை குறி கொண்டு பார்

அப்போது நீ சூரியனை அடைவாய்

Timely Help

55

A help at the right time is much bigger than what it appears to be. It is a life saver to the person in need, though we may not realise it at that time.

Quoting from *Thirukural*, the poet says.

(Poet) காலத்தினால் செய்த நன்றி சிறிதெனிலும்

ஞாலத்தின் மாண பெரிது

(I) A small kind act, at the right time

Is bigger than the world, yours or mine

Good Qualities

The poet notes that people with a high moral standard, even if life hands them hardship, and they seem to fail in life, retain their moral values at all times. On the other hand, people without a moral compass do not remain steadfast to their ideals, and do not remain true friends to others in times of need.

Reading from *Avvaiyar*, the poet says

(*Poet*) அட்டாலும் பால் சுவையிற்குன்றாது - அளவளாய்,

நட்டாலும் நண்பலர் நண்பலரே

கெட்டாலும் மேன் மக்கள் மேன் மக்களே

(I) Great people retain their greatness

In their time of suffering and desolateness

Like how boiled milk retains its taste and whiteness

Like a Mustard

The poet reads about the qualities of the tiny mustard seed. This seed has *allyl isothiocyanate* and many other helpful chemicals inhibitory to dangerous fungi, yeasts and bacteria. Though it is small, the poet uses the mustard seed as an important part of daily cooking as it is common in Tamil cuisine.

The poet looks up from his cooking pan, happy with the taste, and wants us to be like the mustard seed, adding character and spice to whatever we are part of. Size does not matter here.

(Poet) கடுகு சிறுத்தாலும் காட்டம் குறையாது

(I) The little mustard

Retains its character

Giving Wages

The poet notes a labourer sweating hard in the fields doing hard work. At the end of the day, the labourer needs his daily wage, to buy food and necessities for his family.

How should the landlord treat the labourer ?

The poet advises thus. Most labourers live a day to day life, without much savings. Would we allow our own family to go without food ? We need to take care of our labourers in the same way.

(*Poet*) சூரியன் அஸ்தமிக்கும் முன்பே

தொழிலாளிக்கு கூலியை கொடு

(*I*) *You shall give him his wages on his day before the sun sets*

Good Company

It is very difficult to find the traits of a person just by looking at the person. But the poet says, if we know their friends, we can find out what kind of traits the person might have. While not always guaranteed to be true, this simple knowledge can save us from unsavoury situations later.

(Poet) Tell me your friend

I will tell you who you are

(I) உன் நண்பன் யாரென்று சொல்

நீ யாரென்பதை நான் சொல்கிறேன்

The poet also notes that it is sufficient to taste just one morsel of rice, to get a taste of the entire pot. Sometimes, experiencing one incident is enough to understand a person, or a family.

Colloquially, the poet says.

(Poet) ஒரு பானை சோற்றுக்கு, ஒரு சோறு பதம்

(I) A morsel is enough to get the taste of food

(I) But we should be careful enough to avoid developing biases, as one incident may not be sufficient to judge a person.

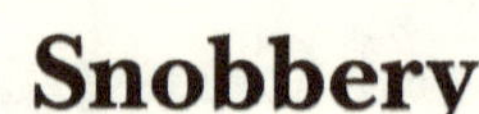

Snobbery

The poet, being well travelled, has seen societies without exception changing with easy availability of money (or credit) and upward mobility of social classes.

In one such instance, over a long period of time, he observes two families who live together on the different floors of a tall house.

They live modestly, as they need each other for help. The poet hears the ladies of the families telling each other.

(Poet) மேல் வீட்டு அச்சியே

நிங்கட்கு நங்களும் வேணும்

நங்கட்கு நிங்களும் வேணும்

(I) You need us, and we need you

The poet observes that after some time, the families become rich, and they forget the past and their bonding, and begin to fight amongst themselves, each treating the other as inferior. And now the poet records them telling each other,

(Poet) மேல் வீட்டு அச்சியே

நிங்கட்கு நங்களும் வேண்டா

நங்கட்கு நிங்களும் வேண்டா

(I) You don't need us, and we don't need you

Saddened by the turn of events, the poet says this about the reality of life.

This is the reason that the poor live happily, with a contented heart, while the rich live a litigated life, trying to protect their turf.

(I) Money brings comfort, but many a time, breaks relations.

Being Strong

The poet sees many of the neighbourhood children getting into friendly fights, particularly while playing with each other. Being patient with many children, he listens intently to such stories as they return from their playing ground. Sharing, give-and-take, is an important philosophy that children need to learn, before their body develops. Being self-confident is a measure of our inner strength.

The poet advises, applying this equally to children and adults,

(Poet) உன் எதிரி உன்னை விழ வைத்தால்

அவனை பின்னுக்கு தள்ளாமலிருக்க

உனக்கு தைரியம் இருக்க வேண்டும்

(I) If your enemy takes you down

You must have the guts, not to push him down

Principles

The poet notes that we are gifted with an inbuilt conscience, however weak it may be. This inbuilt rudder helps us to navigate life's treacherous paths, and its various pressures. But when we are able to surmount troubles without yielding to temptation, we feel a sense of relief, a sense of joy, knowing that we took the right steps.

(Poet) நாம் உண்மையின் பாதையில் நடக்கும் போது

அதனால் நமக்கு துன்பங்கள் நேரும்போது

நாம் கடவுளின் பார்வையில் நேர்த்தியாய் இருக்கிறோம்

என்று மகிழ்ச்சியாயிருப்போம்

(I) When pressures mount because

We walk the path of truth and right

We can rejoice to know that

We are pleasing in God's sight

Having Faith

The poet hears a parent encouraging his child.

(Parent) One day, you will become a great leader!

(Child) But that is impossible! It is so difficult to become a leader. I am not even talented, and I do not have strength

(Parent) But you have to try! We need to attempt and expect great things. Something that pushes us out of our ordinary daily lives, to live extraordinary lives!

The poet underlines the importance of faith, that sometimes we do not need to see everything to believe, and instead should be faithful. We need to make the jump for things to happen. We might fail at the first attempt, but nothing is impossible with perseverance and faith.

(Poet) கடவுளுக்காக பெரிய காரியங்களை செய்

கடவுள் உனக்கு பெரிய காரியங்களை செய்வார்

(I) Attempt great things for God

Expect great things from God

Arrogance

As the poet wanders around the beautiful countryside, he experiences the kindness of people all around, both rich and poor. In one instance, outside a palatial house, he sees the lady of the house feeding a dog.

(I) She is so kind, feeding a stray

The dog has its fill, enjoying the last morsel of food it was fed.

(I) What will the dog do now ? It has partaken the food, and is looking around

Loud growls, and a cry of surprise fill the street.

(I) Oh wait. The dog is trying to chase the Lady, amid loud growls! What more could the dog have wanted ?

The poet describes the situation.

(Poet) அரி தின்னதும் போரா

அம்மையை கடிச்சதும் போரா

பின்னும் பட்டிக்கு தன்ன முறுக்கம்

(I) Sometimes, we help others only to find ourselves being targeted without reason. Remembering this fact of life, will be

useful when dealing with those who are exceedingly difficult to work with, and keep complaining. They keep asking for more, even after enjoying all they got.

Helplessness of the Mighty

The poet hears this story, set around the country in the comfortable confines of a rich ruler, that tells about the helplessness of the rich when faced with little things that cannot be controlled.

A little bird happens to fly over a King/Lord (*Thambiran*)'s palace.

Tired, the bird looks around, and is amazed at the lavish surroundings of the palace, and sets itself on a tree. The surroundings give it an (perhaps false) illusion of being a king.

And then it chances upon a gold coin lying on the ground, and picks up the heavy and shining piece.

Lifting the coin with a struggle, it flies to the nearest pillar and looks around. No one else has a gold coin !!

Feeling proud and richer than ever, the bird begins to harp in a loud voice that can be heard by many.

As the poet walks by, he hears the bird calling out.

(*Bird*) *தம்புரான காட்டிலும் எனிக்காண சம்பத்து*

தம்புரான காட்டிலும் எனிக்காண சம்பத்து

(I) *See all, I am richer than the King*

The king who is in court, hears the shrill voice, and is mortified!

He asks the courtiers to catch the bird and teach it a lesson. The finest of men run out to catch the bird by all means.

True to its name, the bird flies off and seats itself on the highest mast of the palace, and now cries even louder, imagining that the King is out to enrich himself at its expense.

(Bird) தம்புராட்டிக்கொரு தாலி பணிக்கான்

தம்புரான் பொன் பணம் தட்டிப்பறிச்சு

(I) The king wants to make a golden chain for the queen, and is stealing gold from me

The king is even more helpless, and can do nothing but watch, until the bird tires and flies off elsewhere.

The poet notes that, sometimes, even if we are the King, we cannot get everything in life. When facing trivial and unrelated troubles, we just need to let it go and focus on things that matter to us.

Contributing to the Nation

The poet has been transported in a strange vehicle, to a strange land. However, he sees that the vehicle is luxurious, but never seems to move. Wherever he sees, there are vehicles. He learns that this is called a *"traffic jam"*.

He has to listen to his co-passenger for the remaining part of the journey, as the passenger vents out his ire on the ruling class, for the infrastructure issues in their country - bad condition of roads, traffic jam, Pollution etc.

After listening for a while, the poet gets tired of the tirade, and points out that it is them, the ordinary citizens who have the power to make this country proud.

Quoting from *Jean Dreze, the Belgian-Indian Economist,* the poet says.

(Poet) The important task is not so much to find a "new India", but to contribute to making one

And attributing this to *John F Kennedy*, he adds.

(Poet) Ask not what your country can do for you

Ask what you can do for your country,

(I) நாடு எனக்கு என்ன செய்தது என்று கேட்காதே

நாட்டுக்கு நான் என்ன செய்தேன் என்று கேள்

Seven to Avoid

Life is all about decisions. The choices we make when we are at the crossroads, forge new paths in our lives. How do we make these choices ? The poet asks around, and learns the secret.

Understanding the seven things to avoid in life, quoting from *Viveka Chintamani (விவேக சிந்தாமணி)*, the poet says.

(Poet) ஆபத்துக்குதவாத பிள்ளை

அரும்பசிக்கு உதவாத அன்னம்

தாகத்துக்குதவாத தண்ணீர்

தரமறிந்து வாழா பெண்டிர்

கோபத்தை அடக்கா வேந்தன்

குரு மொழி கேடா சீடன்

பாவத்தை தீர்க்கா தீர்த்தம்

பயனில்லை இவை ஏழும் தான்

(I) A child who does not help

Food that does not quench hunger

Water that does not fill thirst

Women who do not understand

King who cannot control anger

Disciple who does not heed his master

Divine stream that does not wash away my sin

These, are seven things to be avoided

(I) Experience speaks.

(I) So, why should a king be able to control himself, why the emphasis on anger ?

The poet answers,

(Poet) ஆத்திரக்காரனுக்கு புத்தி மட்டு

(I) Because he who is angry, has little sense, and cannot make the right decisions.

Living in a
Pluralistic World

The poet meets a person who has just moved in from another part of the world, trying to settle in. He advises the person to follow what others do in the community and be together with them.

(Poet) ஊருடன் ஒத்து வாழ்

Quoting from the Sangam poet *Kaniyan Poongunranar,* from the book *Purananooru (புறநானூறு),* he says,

(Poet) யாதும் ஊரே யாவரும் கேளிர்

(I) Every place is our own, everyone is our friend

This attribute of trying to communicate with others at their level, can sometimes slow down social progress and exacerbate biases and ignorance, particularly when the masses mingle. A just way that accommodates everyone's needs is indeed hard to find, but worth working towards in harmony.

(I) When in Rome, do as the Romans do

Many times we act inappropriately, especially when interacting with people from other cultures . We can avoid unintended repercussions by knowing the customs of the land, or by learning from others, or just by observing.

The poet says, quoting from Tamil proverbs.

(Poet) செத்தவன் கையிலே வெற்றிலை கொடுத்தது போல

(I) Like giving a leaf to a dead man

(I) We should apologise, and not repeat the mistake again

Do we lose anything by giving in to the reasonable demands of others ? No. But we might lose many things, by remaining adamant and not listening to others.

The poet asks us to be considerate towards others.

(Poet) விட்டு கொடுத்தவன் கெட்டு போவதில்லை

கெட்டு போகிறவன் விட்டு கொடுப்பதில்லை

(I) He who gives in will never lose

He who will lose will never give in

Lending

The poet sees a man, who is in a predicament. He lent money to his friend, thinking it will be returned later. However, it has not yet been returned.

Should he ask him back ?

The poet knows where this will lead. He quotes from the Tamil proverbs.

(Poet) கொடுத்ததை கேட்டால் அடுத்தது பகை

(I) Asking to return what is owed

Without a doubt, enmity is sowed

(I) Though the giving happened in good faith, it leads to hate between the two parties.

When someone keeps delaying repaying his dues for payment (for ex a past loan), it is an indication they do not have the means to pay. But how do we know ?

The poet says, quoting from Tamil proverbs.

(Poet) இன்றில்லை நாளை என்பது

இல்லையென்பதற்கு அடையாளம்

(I) If it is not available tomorrow, and day by day,

Remember, he is never going to repay

Finding Faults

The poet sees a person in the King's court, always pointing out the mistakes of others, and who keeps looking out for such mistakes. Unfortunately, with this habit, the courtier has lost all friends.

The poet advises the lonely Courtier, quoting from a Tamil proverb.

(Poet) குற்றம் பார்க்கின் சுற்றம் இல்லை

(I) If we see everyone falling short

No one will remain our cohort

Help Yourself Before Others

A man has come to see the poet. He blames his past for all his troubles, and without helping himself, he continues to fall at others feet. The poet chastises him and says this. "We may be born financially poor, and we admittedly have no choice there. But there is no excuse for us to continue to be financially poor till the end of our lives!"

The poet quotes this from a colloquial saying.

(Poet) தனக்கு தவிடு இடிக்கமாட்டான்

தம்புரானுக்கு இரும்பு அடிப்பான்

(I) *He who does not want to grind his own rice and bran*

Wants to make iron for the rich man

Another group of people seem lazy and waste their time. The poet admonishes them.

(Poet) ஊனுக்கு ராஜாளி

வேலைக்கு நோயாளி

(I) *He who is an eager eagle when eating food and picking the fork*

Becomes a patient when called for work

Away from Trouble

The poet watches a person trying to negotiate with another, who seems to be intent only on creating a commotion, without actually solving the problem at hand. He likens the troublemaker to a mad elephant, and advises thus.

The poet says this, quoting from *Neethi Venpa* (நீதி வெண்பா).

(*Poet*) வெம்பு கரிக்கு ஆயிரம் (முழம்) தான் வேண்டுமே

வம்பு செய் தீங்கினர் தம் கண் முன் நில்லாததே நலம்

(I) *Like Standing a thousand (muzham) distance away from a mad tusker*

Stand far away from a trouble maker

Helping Others

When helping others in need, we should not even think about when the person might be able to repay us. The poet quotes from *Avvaiyar*.

(Poet) நன்றி ஒருவற்கு செய்தக்கால் அந்நன்றி

என்று தரும் கொல் என வேண்டா

நின்று தளரா வளர் தெங்கும்

தாளுண்ட நீரைத் தலையாலே தான் தருவதால்

(I) If you give to another

Getting it back should not be your bother

For like a precious palm tree

Growing endlessly

You will touch the sky from your root

With boundless sweetness, like tender fruit

Unjust World

The poet sees a person worrying about the increasing evil and injustice in this world. He asks, *"Where is God? Why can't I see justice being delivered right now ?"*.

In answer, the poet glorifies God, quoting from the Tamil proverbs, asking the person not to worry.

(*Poet*) அரசன் அன்று கேட்பான்

தெய்வம் நின்று கேட்கும்

(I) A king is so powerful, that he can claim justice the same day itself.

But a God is even more powerful and can wait across an infinite time, until justice is done.

The poet also quotes from the poet *Nakkeerar*, indicating, there is no escape from injustice, even if done by God himself. We have to call it out, just like *Nakkeerar* does. In this case, the angry God even opened his third eye (of destruction) in a rage when Nakkeerar pointed out his mistake. But Nakkeerar remains unfazed.

(*Poet*) நெற்றிக்கண் திறப்பினும் குற்றம் குற்றமே.

(I) Injustice is injustice, even if it is the very God that did it.

Whom to Help

We may be kind, but sometimes others take us for granted and ask for needless help, or misuse the help provided, taking advantage of our kindness. We need to know if the person or the cause to whom we show our kindness is really worth it.

The poet advises, quoting from the Tamil proverbs.

(Poet) பாத்திரம் அறிந்து பிச்சை போடு

(I) Know the plate before placing alms in it

Impressions

When meeting somebody for the first time, it is easy to believe first impressions, and take their words as true. But later on, we might realise that our understanding was wrong and the words and deeds were false, meant merely to allure us, much like shopping in a discount store. Hence we need to be careful when working with people.

As the poet says, Do not judge a book by its cover!

(*Poet*) வெளுத்ததெல்லாம் பாலல்ல

மின்னுவதெல்லாம் பொன்னல்ல

(*I*) *All that is white is not milk*

All that glitters is not gold or its ilk

Anger of a Quiet Man

A sage is normally seen to be devoid of emotions. But when the sage is made to suffer, he can fully exhibit the true extent of his anger, and at that time, even the big forest cannot accommodate his rage.

The poet says, quoting from the Tamil proverbs.

(Poet) சாது மிரண்டால் காடு கொள்ளாது

(I) Anger of a sage, cannot be contained

The Other Side

The poet observes an animal looking for a place to graze, and as it raises its head, it sees beyond the river with a longing writ large on its face. The other side always looks green and inviting. But the animal misses out on the green grass on its side.

The poet says, similarly, we may tend to ignore the riches we have on this side of the river, and always view something we do not have, with envy. We should avoid such complacency and look for being content with and making the most of what we have.

(Poet) இக்கரைக்கு அக்கரைப் பச்சை

(I) The other side of the river is always green

Know the Depth

The poet sees a man attempting to cross an overflowing river. Before he jumps, he catches him and asks him if he knows the depth of the river, or if he knows swimming. He admonishes him since he knows neither, and is foolish enough to venture into the river.

The poet notes, before venturing into the unknown, or dipping into a dark river bank, understand its true depth. Else we might sink to death.

Quoting a Tamil proverb, the poet says.

(*Poet*) ஆழம் அறிந்து காலை வை

(*I*) *Look before you leap*

Cues

An elephant walks very quietly. The poet imagines the big animal suddenly appearing in the midst of the neighbourhood, walking among people. A bell (tied around the neck) announces to everyone that a tusker is nearby, perhaps to avoid injuries and conflicts and scaring children.

The poet notes in today's context, there are many people who announce their arrival, or events related to them, accompanied by high decibel announcements. When it becomes a pattern, it can be likened to the bell announcing the arrival of the majestic animal.

Taking from the Tamil proverbs, the poet says,

(Poet) ஆனை வரும் பின்னே

மணியோசை வரும் முன்னே

(I) The bell announces first

The elephant arrives next

Cleanliness

87

The poet always washes himself after a hard day's work before sitting for dinner. He notes that whether we are poor or rich, whether eating a sumptuous food or a watery gruel, we must keep our bodies clean before consuming food.

He notes, quoting from the Tamil proverbs.

(Poet) கூழானாலும் குளித்து குடி

(I) Even if eating simple

Eat after a bath

Simplicity

The poet sees traders surrounding themselves with armed guards, when crossing thick forests. They have a lot of money or goods, and they might face thieves in the forest. They have to be ready to defend them.

But he sees simple people who have nothing to lose, travelling without a care, enjoying the wayside.

Those who have gathered money and worldly riches, fear losing them, and die trying hard to protect them.

The poet says.

(*Poet*) மடியில் கனம் இல்லையென்றால்

வழியில் பயம் இல்லை

(*I*) *Those who are poor, live without fear*

Too Much

Even if it is *"Amutham"* (or Amirtham, a divine food eaten by/fit for Gods), consuming it beyond a limit becomes poison. For all the gluttons out there, this should be a warning!

The poet says.

(Poet) அளவுக்கு மீறினால் அமுதமும் நஞ்சு

(I) Even the Amirtham may be poison

When partaken without limit or reason

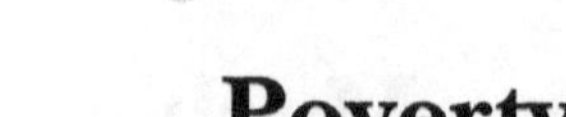

Poverty

When a man is poor and has nothing, no one wants him. Not even his family.

The poet says we should fend for our necessities, without depending on others, without a sense of self-pity.

(Poet) இல்லாதவனை இல்லாளும் வேண்டாள்

ஈன்றெடுத்த தாயும் வேண்டாள்

(I) For those with nothing

There is no waiting wife, no wanting mother

The poet also notes the value of kindness, even if others do not value us. if we do not have wealth, the whole world ignores us, as if we do not exist. All decisions appear to be taken without taking us into account.

But if we do not have kindness or empathy towards others, the next world (ie, after death) will ignore us.

The poet says, we need to be conscious of our responsibilities towards the downtrodden, quoting from the book, *Thirukural.*

(Poet) பொருளில்லார்க்கு இவ்வுலகம் இல்லை

அருளில்லார்க்கு அவ்வுலகம் இல்லை

(I) Not for us, this world, those who have nothing

And not the next, for those who are not kind

Reading *Thirukural,* the poet adds, we need to be available to others and help others in their time of need, and not live an isolated life that ignores the fate of others. Like the neurons that criss-cross and connect various parts of our body, we are all connected together in some way.

(Poet) அன்பிலார் என்றும் தமக்குரியர்

அன்புடையார் என்பும் உரியர் பிறற்கு

(I) Those without love, belong to themselves

Those who love others, belong to all

Busybody

The poet sees that the illusion of motion is alluring to many people. When they have nothing to do, life feels idle, and unapologetically they end up doing stale and unimportant things. But to someone looking from outside, it looks like they are busy, and they are satisfied with that perception of the outside world.

The poet notes, idle people often look busy, but accomplish nothing.

(Poet) நாய்க்கு ஒரு வேலையுமில்லை

உட்காந்திருக்க நேரமுமில்லை

(I) The dog has little to do

And little time to rest

What goes Around

The poet notes that there are always after-effects to every action, particularly ones involving interaction with others, when we have to take some drastic steps. It could be cutting off a relationship, filing lawsuits in the hope for justice, or moving our place of living.

For any of these actions, the poet advises we need to be prepared to bear the after-effects that will hit us as surely as the rising of the sun.

The poet says.

(Poet) நாயை அடிப்பானேன், பீயை சுமப்பானேன்

(I) If you beat a dog to death, be ready to carry its remains

(I) If you pray for the rain, be ready for the mud as well

Empty Vessel

The poet is asked by the crafty courtiers, to identify which of the vessels placed before him, is filled with water. The poet knows, a vessel filled to the brim with brim, will not thrash around even if moved or hit, because it is heavy. He uses this knowledge to identify the full vessel.

Likewise, a wise person will not be perturbed even if treated badly, and remains focused on goals.

The poet says.

(Poet) நிறை குடம் தழும்பாது

(I) A full vessel never makes sound

Watch the Tongue

We should take care of what we speak, and when. Else we might end up like a frog that gets eaten by other predators, because it could not stop croaking, and hence announces its location to its enemies.

Once we speak a word, the word and its effects become intractable, and remain permanent in this world.

The poet advises,

(*Poet*) தவளை தன் வாயால் கெடும்

(*I*) *A frog is given away by its mouth*

The poet observes that, in addition to what we speak, we should also be mindful of what we think and do.

(*Poet*) தன் வினை

தன்னைச்சுடும்

(*I*) *Evil actions*

Come back to haunt us

Two Minded

The poet observes a person who seems to be dilly-dallying about, when trying to accomplish a task. He asks, "Confidence in action can only be achieved if everything is planned adequately. Have you planned?".

Be confident while taking the step forward, not with two minds.

The poet says.

(Poet) ஆத்துல ஒரு கால், சேத்துல ஒரு கால்

(I) Like having a leg in the river

And another in the river-bank

Rain

97

It is monsoon season, and the clouds have opened up. The poet observes a person waiting for the rains to let up.

Monsoon rains mostly start in the evening, and it keeps pouring through the night. A naive person thinks that the rain will stop, but it never does.

The poet advises the person to not wait for the rain to stop, but to continue forward with the task at hand.

(Poet) அந்தி மழை அழுதாலும் விடாது

(I) The evening rain never stops even if we cry

The River Cauvery

Long ago, the river Cauvery was the lifeline to the entire delta region in the south of India, as it went on its way to the ocean through the plains. It was never dry, and was always flowing, unlike today's times when it swells only during the monsoon, or when the Mettur and Krishna Raja Sagara dams open their shutters.

The poet records this, going back and forth across the pages of history, underlying the important connection between humankind and the environment.

The poet notes, we must nurture and take care of our environment.

(Poet) வானம் பொய்த்தாலும்

தான் பொய்யா காவேரி

(I) Even if the clouds fail

The river Cauvery never fails

Like Salt

Salt is well known as a preservative, as well as for making food tasty, and humans need salt in measured quantities for their well-being. The poet notes that food without salt has no taste and cannot be preserved as well.

(Poet) உப்பில்லா பண்டம் குப்பையிலே

(I) Food without salt, ends up in the garbage

In the Gene

The poet listens to a story from a well-heeled traveller, with stories of how tigers hunt. He learns that highly evolved species do not change their traits even for a short time, just to satisfy their short-term instincts. They lie in wait, knowing their time will come.

Patience and focus are key in the game of survival.

The poet says.

(Poet) புலி பசித்தாலும் புல்லை தின்னாது

(I) A tiger, even if hungry

will never eat grass though so shiny

Health and Speech

As the poet goes about his morning rituals, he beautifully compares strengths. The strength of the well maintained teeth, and the strength of our speech.

(Poet) ஆலும் வேலும் பல்லுக்குறுதி

நாலும் இரண்டும் சொல்லுக்குறுதி

(I) Banyan and Neem sticks strengthen the teeth

Verses from Naladiyar (four) and Thiruvalluvar (two) strengthen the speech

(*Thiruvalluvar* wrote couplets, and *Naladiyar* wrote verses with four lines)

The human speech production system involves a complex combination of the vocal cords, tongue, teeth and lips. When teeth are lost, speech is lost because the lips tend to sag and cannot form legible words, particularly involving consonants.

The poet advises us to take care of our teeth.

(Poet) பல் போனால் சொல் போச்சு

(I) If teeth is lost

Speech is lost

(I) A painting can be drawn only if there is a wall (canvas). Without a canvas, even if we have beautiful colours, we cannot draw, and our imagination is stilted.

Similarly, we need to keep our bodies strong to do useful things. Even if we have a great mind and thoughts, we need a healthy body to translate our thoughts into actions. The mind can only make its presence felt through the actions of a physical entity.

The poet notes this, with a quote from Tamil proverbs.

(Poet) சுவர் இருந்தால் தான் சித்திரம் எழுத முடியும்

(I) Only if there is a canvas, can we draw

Empty Words

The poet is hungry, and searches the vessel for more food. All he hears is the wooden spoon scraping against the vessel.

Annoyed, the poet notes that food will be in the spoon, only if there is food left in the vessel. Else the spoon will come out empty.

The verse indicates the empty nature of people can easily be identified, by the words they speak, or their actions.

(Poet) பானையில் இருந்தால்

அகப்பையில் வரும்

(I) If food is in the vessel

It will come in the spoon

Being Too Careful

The poet is invited to an animal trade fair, an annual event in the countryside. As he watches, a trader gets lucky and gets a free animal, perhaps from a friendly trader, or as a result of a competition, as the fair gets to a close. In such a situation, it is foolish for a person to verify the quality of the animal, for example by checking every aspect of its teeth in detail. He should take it and profit from it.

The poet notes this informally.

(*Poet*) இலவசமா கிடைச்ச மாட்டுக்கு

பல் புடுங்கி பாத்தானாம் ஒருத்தன்

(I) *Do not check the teeth of a buffalo, when you get it for free*

(I) *Make hay while the sun shines*

Vanity

A person is too proud of himself, and the poet sees that several outcomes of this trait are hilarious. The poet observes this when someone trips and falls. The person ensures his most precious possessions do not get soiled, particularly when others are watching. The actions of a person when falling, indicate clearly the aspects that the person intends to protect.

The poet says, quoting from Tamil proverbs.

(*Poet*) விழுந்தாலும் மீசையில் மண் ஒட்டாமல் காத்தது போல

(*I*) *Like keeping the moustache clean even after falling into the dust*

Difficult Things

The poet meets a person who never listens to advice and remains stubbornly attached to his own thinking. He likens this to blowing a conch to the ear of a person who is deaf. It is futile to try to change their mindset. It is better to leave them to their own fate, until realisation dawns on them.

The poet says, quoting from the Tamil proverbs.

(*Poet*) செவிடன் காதில் ஊதிய சங்கு போல

(*I*) *Like blowing a conch to a deaf person*

The poet also relates this task to an impossible feat, visualising it in a colourful fashion.

(*Poet*) ஊசியின் காதில்

ஒட்டகத்தை நுழைப்பது போல்

(*I*) *Like pushing a camel*

Through the eye of a needle

The poet notes that the stiff nature of our characters, once imbibed, is too hard to change, making it an impossible task.

(*Poet*) நாய் வாலை நிமிர்த்த முடியுமா?

(*I*) *Can we straighten a dog's tail ?*

Many people do not listen to suggestions or requests from others, but keep going as if they did not see or hear anything, ignoring the others. Some children do not obey their elders.

The poet likens this behaviour to that of an animal. When it rains, humans usually run for cover. But a thick skinned animal like a buffalo does not even flinch, and continues its grazing, ignoring the rain.

(Poet) எருமை மாட்டின் மேல்

மழை பெய்தது போல்

(I) Like the rain

Falling on a buffalo

Paying More

The poet meets a trader, who is arguing with a transporter, very surprised at the amount he has to pay for transport of a vegetable. This verse illustrates his outburst, frustrated at his loss. The currency (*Panam*), might refer to an "*Anna*", that was the equivalent of 1/16 th of a current day *Rupee*.

Sometimes we end up spending more on transporting the material, than the value of the material itself.

The poet understands this anomaly, and quotes from the Tamil proverbs.

(*Poet*) சுண்டக்காய் முக்கா பணம்

சுமை கூலி மூணு பணம்

(I) The Turkey-berry costs 3/4 anna

But the transport costs 3 anna

(I) The Turkey-berry, the fruit of the plant Solanum torvum, also called Sundakkai in Tamil, is widely consumed as a vegetable in the South of India, and has proven medicinal benefits

Life Events

After a major life event, the poet looks back and sees what happened. The situation appears to overcome him and has taken a big toll on him. Perhaps he has lost someone to disease, or an unforeseen event. Hopelessness is in the air. This verse describes how the poet feels indifferent to life, overburdened with grief and fatigue.

(*Poet*) தலைக்கு மேலே போனதுக்கப்புறம்

சாண் போனா என்ன

முழம் போனா என்ன

(I) *Head under water*

Who cares

If it is higher by an inch

Or one feet

But the poet is not one who gives up easily. He is able to emerge triumphant after all the tribulations, and is now happy. A sense of worry and a simultaneous sense of relief pervades him. This verse captures him in this state of precarious apprehension.

(*Poet*) தலைக்கு வந்தது தலைப்பாகையோடு போயிற்று

(I) *What came for the head, left with the turban*

Handling Grief

In earlier pages, the poet talks about the love a mother has for her child.

When *Avvaiyar's* mother is asked to abandon her child and move on to another place, the poetess consoles herself (and her mother) with these timeless words. A sense of irony pervades the verse, but ends with a positive burst, by placing all the troubles in the feet of God, to lead a fearless life. We need to teach our children to live a fearless life.

The poet quotes from Avvaiyar (ஒளவையார்), who is addressing this to herself, and her mother.

(Poet) இட்ட முடன் என் தலையில் இன்னபடி என்றெழுதி

விட்ட சிவனும் செத்துவிட்டானோ?

முட்ட முட்ட பஞ்சமே ஆயினும்

பாரம் அவனுக்கே

நெஞ்சமே அஞ்சாதே நீ

(I) Did he vanish, this Creator ?

Who stamped on my forehead, it is what it is

He who wrote my fate

Will also bear its weight

My heart, do not be afraid

A Helping Hand

In times of difficulties, we fall into the trap of a "victim mindset" and our troubles overcome us, as we wallow in self-pity. But what of others, who are in a more difficult position than us ? When we think or read of struggles that others have faced, our own difficulties may pale and we feel more stronger. This is one of the benefits of reading widely, and gaining more perspective, instead of focusing on ourselves.

We should help others who are in need more than us.

(Poet) காலில் செருப்பில்லையே என்றழுதேன்

காலில்லாதோரை காணும் வரை

(I) I cried that I did not have a shoe

Until I met one who did not have a foot too

A Poet's Agony

While the royal poets at the King's court live a royal life, under the patronage of the King, the poet meets many others, who struggle to make a living.

He meets one such compatriot, angry at his situation. Why did God make him a poet, he asks. The poet says, quoting from இராமச்சந்திரக் கவிராயர்,

(Poet) கல்லைத்தான், மண்ணைத்தான், காய்த்துதான்

குடிக்கத்தான் கற்பித்தானா? அன்றி

இல்லைத்தான் பொன்னைத் தான் எனக்குத் தான்

கொடுத்துத்தான் இருப்பித் தானா?

பல்லைத் தான் மூடத்தான் பயமாய்த்தான் இருக்கத்தான்

பதுமத்தான் படைத்திட்டானே

(I) The Lotus one (the creator)

Did he teach me to live on

A potion of boiled stone and mud, and go on ?

Or did he settle me with golden gifts and myrrh?

Alas, a (false) smile to show my teeth,

Is all, the Lotus one (the creator), blessed me with,

Another poet is angry that his stomach goes hungry again and again without fail, every time of the day, and every day. He feels distinct from the biological function and necessity of eating, and gives it a mouthful.

The poet quotes this gem, from the *Neethi Venpa (நீதி வெண்பா), a collection of songs.*

(*Poet*) ஒரு நாள் உணவை ஒழியென்றால் ஒழியாய்

இரு நாளுக்கும் ஏல் என்றாய் ஏலாய்

ஒரு நாளும் என் நோவு அறியாய்

இடும்பை கூறு என் வயிறே

உன்னோடு வாழ்தல் அரிது

(I) You will not tolerate hunger for a day

You will not store food for two days

You will never understand my pain

Oh Stomach, that lives with me,

It is difficult to live with you

The poet, though poor himself, sees on many occasions where money opens seemingly non-existent doors for him. There is no avenue that will not open, if enough money is on the table.

The poet says.

(*Poet*) பணம் என்றால் பிணமும் வாய் திறக்கும்

(I) Even a corpse will open its mouth, if shown money

The Sunken Eyes

This verse exhorts the reader to not worry unnecessarily, as if addressed to the general populace. A deeper and alternate meaning emerges on a closer look. Focusing on the words "sunken eyes" hits the reader with a new perspective, shining the light on the plight of the everyday life of the poor and downtrodden. They have but a four foot loin cloth and much suffering for company, and worry themselves to death thinking of many useless things.

The poet takes this from *Avvaiyar's* writings.

(*Poet*) உண்பது நாழி

உடுப்பது நான்கு முழம்

எண்பது கோடி எண்ணி நினைந்து வாடுவன

கண் புதைந்த மாந்தர்க்கு

வாழ்க்கை, மண்ணின் கலம் போல

சாகுந்தனையும் சஞ்சலம் தான்

(I) Eating a measured meal daily

Draped in four foot

Eighty crore thoughts lashing the mind

For those with sunken eyes

Life, is but a mud vessel

With tears till the end

A Dead End

The poet encounters a person who has many options to choose from, but still cannot act on any of those options. This verse illustrates a situation when we have no way out, or when left with few options to choose from, none of them palatable to us.

The poet says, quoting from the Tamil proverbs,

(*Poet*) இருதலைக் கொள்ளி எறும்பு போல

(*I*) *Like an ant stuck between fires burning on all sides*

(*I*) *Caught between the devil and the deep sea*

(*I*) *If one is strong enough, with focus and hard work, there is always a way to be found.*

Wandering Life

The sea is vast and expands all the way to the horizon. When it is windy, wave after wave comes crashing to the shore. The waves pick up floating pieces of garbage and deposit them on the shore. But we cannot locate something that falls into the sea. It is almost impossible, especially if it is small like a piece of iron.

Sometimes life throws us around, like a nail thrown in a sea. We fail to find purpose, as if it is lost.

The poet says, about this seeming lack of purpose.

(Poet) அலை கடல் துரும்பு போல

(I) Like a piece lost in the boiling sea

(I) We need guidance at this time, and we should seek it with a purpose

Fear

When an animal gets hurt, its first reaction is to hide or run. During this time, it fears everything in its path. Even a firefly, a relatively tiny insect, can scare it. This verse talks specifically about a cat that is branded, but it could be true of larger species, and humans as well.

It takes a really long time to recover from a tragic life event. Often, irrecoverable.

(Poet) கொள்ளி அடிபட்ட பூனைக்கு

மின்னிட்டான் பூச்சியைப்பார்த்தும் பயம்

(I) A cat branded with a hot iron pike

Fears even a firefly for it too burns bright

In a similar manner, a person who is already scared, sees a ghost in every darkness.

(Poet) அரண்டவன் கண்ணுக்கு இருண்டதெல்லாம் பேய்

(I) For one who is scared

In everything dark is a ghost to be dared

The heart rate of a person who has something to hide, tends to be higher than normal, or skips a beat. This fact is used in lie-detectors, and this simple verse just reflects this reality.

The poet says.

(Poet) குற்றம் செய்த நெஞ்சம் குறுகுறுக்கும்

(I) The heart of a sinner

Always flutters

The poet expresses the situation of a borrower, who lives in a perennial fear of not being able to repay his debt.

(Poet) கடன் பட்டார் நெஞ்சம் போல்

(I) Like the heartbeat of men

Who owe others ten

Troubles

Many circumstances in life are effervescent, like the bloom of a flower. The flower blooms in the morning, and withers away by dusk or gets blown away by the wind. It is not something of permanence. Likewise, we need to live in the hope that our troubles are temporary, and will get over soon.

(*Poet*) அன்றலர்ந்த மலர் போல்

(*I*) *Like a withering flower at dusk*

This next verse illustrates a comparison with the dew. In the early morning, the dew is visible clearly, settled down peacefully on the grass and leaves. But once the sun rises, the dew evaporates and is not seen anymore. Similarly, problems in life go away at their time, and are no longer visible.

The poet says this about our troubles. They are short lived, and we should live a life of hope. For hope is better than fear, and love is better than war.

(*Poet*) சூரியனை கண்ட பனி போல்

(*I*) *Like the dew that vanishes at the sight of the sun*

Life Moves On

Nearing the end of his journey, the poet hears the strangest experience of a blind person.

"They say, the life of a blind person is hard. But I never know what I am missing. I live in a world of my own, content in my own right. But imagine when one fine day, I am granted the gift of sight. The whole world becomes colourful, a flood of new sensations envelopes me, and I am overjoyed at seeing this wonderful world." The man stops, and a tear emerges in his sightless eyes. He composes himself, and continues.

"Just as suddenly, if the gift is taken away again, wouldn't I feel a lot of pain ? Something that I didn't know existed was revealed to me, then taken away again."

The poet describes his pain, taking from the poet *Kambar's* writings in *Kamba Ramayanam*.

(கம்பர்) கண்ணில்லான் பெற்றிழந்தான் எனவுழந்தான்

கடுந்துயரம் கால வேலான்

(I) The blind man cries

Not because now he cannot see

But once before, he knew what it meant to be

Not just hear and touch, but to feel and see

In darkness he tries to see again but in vain

O cruel timekeeper, thou has cast unbearable pain

The poet notes how the world has turned for the person, from one extreme to another. Perhaps it happened in a very short time. But the memory of that experience sticks with him forever. He wants to see again, to see and feel together with the brightness of the world again but cannot. What a pity !

The Sangam poet *Kaniyan Poongunranar* (கணியன் பூங்குன்றனார்) says during such trying times, instead of living with self-pity loaded with extremes of emotions that can overwhelm us, live with the calm understanding that everything is a part of life. A higher order of understanding is required, and it takes time to inculcate this in our lives.

The poet says.

(*Poet*) இன்று என மகிழ்ந்தன்றும் இலமே

(*I*) *Do not be overjoyed when the good was had,*

and do not be sad for something bad

The poet also notes the tendency of people to blame others when things go wrong. He advises not to do it, and stresses the need to flow with the stream of life, without blaming anyone or anything, including God or others, or even ourselves.

The poet says, quoting from *Kaniyan Poongunranar* again.

(*Poet*) தீதும் நன்றும் பிறர் தர வாரா

(*I*) *What comes to us, good or bad, is not because of others deeds*

The poet adds his final thoughts.

(*Poet*) It is what it is.

I am not the first one who faces pain, and I definitely am not the last. Life moves on, and so should I.

Do good deeds without expecting a return and live a life without regrets.